# Loving

Spiritual Exercises in Tangibly
Loving Your Literal Neighbors

Tim Nichols and Joe Anderson

Published by Headwaters Christian Resources
P.O. Box 175, Englewood, CO 80151

Loving

Copyright © 2016, Timothy Nichols and Joseph Anderson.

All rights reserved. Printed in the United States of America. No part of this book may be used or reproduced in any manner whatsoever without written permission except in the case of brief quotations embodied in critical articles or reviews.


ISBN-13:978-1-945413-82-7

10 9 8 7 6 5 4 3 2 1

# CONTENTS

How to Use this Book......................................................5
1. Trusting Jesus' Way: Theory and Theology....................7
2. Tangible Love: How to do Basic Neighboring................17
3. Growing in Love: Spiritual Friendship and Leadership..37
Occasional Articles........................................................53

## How To Use This Book

Of course you can read this book straight through, and we encourage you to. It won't take that long.

But it's your book, and you can do whatever you want. So if you just can't wait to get started, go straight to Chapter 2 and use the checklist to have your first neighborhood barbecue tonight. If you're going to do that, though, please promise me that you won't invite anybody to church. Seriously. Why shouldn't you? Well, for that you're going to have to read Chapter 1.

So don't get stuck in Chapter 2 forever. Neighboring is the kind of thing where you have to do some improvising, and you'll do your best improvising when you really understand what you're trying to accomplish. So once you've got your barbecue plans rolling, come back and read the rest. Chapter 1 will give you a big-picture grasp of neighboring, and that will help you improvise effectively and keep you from getting frustrated if things don't work out quite the way you planned them. Chapter 3 will help you grow from just being a fun neighbor to being a good neighbor. The articles will give you some other angles of approach to neighboring.

May God bless you with the love of the Father, the peace of Christ, and the comfort of the Spirit—enough to fill you to overflowing, that out of your belly will flow rivers of living water.

# 1

# Trusting Jesus' Way: Theory and Theology of Neighboring

## How We Got Started

In 2008, my wife and I moved to Englewood, Colorado, eager to start our lives together. We had jobs, a place to live... all we thought we lacked was a church. We didn't want to waste our time "church shopping," so we prayed that God would lead us to the church where He wanted us to be and make it a place of rich community life for us. We wanted our church to be our primary community.

God answered the first part of our prayer: that we would be in the church He had for us. We found a church to attend and not long after, they hired me as associate pastor. It was a great fit. But, in His infinite wisdom, God simply didn't allow that church to become a rich source of community life. We had friends there, but the family-like community we hoped for never happened.

Meanwhile, we got to know our next-door neighbors. We didn't share a religious commitment with them, but we did share a backyard fence and had kids about the same age. They became some of our closest friends and remain so to this day (though both of our families have moved since then). Over time, we became friends with other neighbors, and eventually identified our block as our primary source of community life.

Finding community among our neighbors was a gift from God... it *happened* to us. We didn't set out to love our neighbors (like we should have—we're Christians after all), but God gave us a love for them. One day it occurred to us that we had fallen into biblical obedience. Furthermore, we realized that we had lacked basic obedience to the second most important command in the Bible for pretty much our entire lives. *We had never learned to love our literal neighbors.*

This realization changed us. From that day on, we made it our aim to become experts at loving our neighbors.

## Why Emphasize Neighboring?

Because Jesus said to. And it won't do to say, "I don't have time for my literal neighbors, but I love the 'neighbors' I work with and the 'neighbors' on my kids' sports teams." Yes, we should be good neighbors to everyone God puts in our path. But we all know that it's hypocrisy to love your church "family" and neglect your literal family. The same is true of neighboring. It's hypocrisy to love your figurative neighbors and neglect your literal neighbors.

Loving your neighbor is both a straightforward command and God's chosen metaphor for all relationships. As a straightforward command, we are supposed to love our neighbors (people who live nearby) as ourselves. As a metaphor, we are supposed to love everyone we come across as though they were our neighbors.

Loving your neighbor is the master metaphor for relationships because it doesn't lend itself to setting boundaries. Are your neighbors just the people who share a property line? Just the people on your block, or in your apartment complex? Yes and yes, as well as the person you share the road and the elevator with. Of course some guy who lives in Omaha isn't your neighbor if you live in Denver...unless you happen to be traveling through Omaha or you're talking with him on the phone for some reason or another. Your neighbors are those who are near—if you're in contact with the person, then he's your neighbor.

It's important to love your literal neighbor; not just because it's part of the command, but because learning to love your literal neighbors well trains you to love everyone well. You choose a lot of the people in your life, but you don't choose your neighbors. You just have to love whoever happens to live next door. If you make a habit of ignoring the people who live next door, do you think you will love the checker in the grocery line (who also happens to be easy to ignore)? How about your kid's soccer coach, or teacher, or the homeless person you happen to walk past on your way to work? We are creatures of habit, and we train ourselves to notice and love people by loving our literal neighbors.

Biblically speaking, your relationships to your neighbors are the primary human relationships. You might notice that Jesus did not say loving your spouse or your kids was the second most important commandment. Your immediate family (if you live with them) are your closest neighbors, and everything out from there is an extension of your call to love your neighbors.

Of course, life isn't so simple that we can say if you fail to love your literal neighbors, you will fail to love others. There are certainly people who don't love their literal neighbors but are doing a bang-up job loving the homeless. But, as a general principle, loving your literal neighbors will tend to push you outward and make you a more loving person in every area of life. Also, it's where God said to start. So there's that.

---

**Spiritual Exercise #1: Learn Their Names**

It's difficult to love people who live next to you if you don't learn their names. Start with the people who live immediately around you—on either side, across the street, across the back fence or alley. Or if you live in an apartment, the unit across the hall and the units you share a common wall, floor or ceiling with. Go find out what their names are. DON'T DO ANYTHING ELSE. Don't invite them to church, don't try to evangelize them, none of that. Not yet. Don't be weird; just introduce yourself and learn their names. Write them down and put the paper on your refrigerator, so you'll remember. Assign a day of the week to each household, and pray for them on that day, so you will pray for all your nearest neighbors by name at least once a week.

## The Neighboring Mindset

There are lots of things you can do to be a good neighbor, but it's important to distinguish between the ministry vehicles (stuff you do) and the heart of the matter. Having a barbecue or cleaning someone's gutters are nice things to do, but *being present with your neighbors and tangibly loving them*—that's what neighboring actually *is*. Cleaning gutters is just a vehicle, one of many ways to neighbor.

It's important to get your head around this concept, because vehicles come and go. You might have morning coffee on Saturday, and people come and hang out for three months, and then attendance dwindles and pretty soon nobody comes. If you're starting a coffee shop, that's a disaster—but you're not starting a coffee shop. Were you able to tangibly love your neighbors with good coffee and conversation during those three months? Yes. So that's a win. Now that your neighbors aren't coming around for coffee every Saturday, are you going to be unable to love them? Don't be silly. You're hardly limited to serving coffee on Saturdays; there are tons of other ways to love your neighbors. So don't worry. Once you get the hang of this, vehicles are a dime a dozen. When one has run its course, drop it and find more.

Which brings us to another key point: neighboring is a long-term endeavor. You aren't trying to get it all done this weekend. Some neighbors may become fast friends. Others may take a long time to warm up to you. You're in no hurry. Later this year, something will happen that opens the door. Or next year. Or the year after. God is not stymied by your neighbors' shyness or antisocial tendencies; why should you fret about it? Relax. Take your time. God is in no hurry—why should you be?

Now in reality, you aren't going to be willing to take your time unless you adjust your scorecard a bit. Learn to celebrate *all* the victories. What would your neighborhood look like if it were transported into the fully-realized kingdom of God, when heaven has come to earth and the New Jerusalem is the capital of the world? That glorious reality is coming. Our goal is to anticipate that future in your neighborhood now. Any movement toward the kingdom counts as success. Seriously, *anything*.

We have a tendency to only count the "big" things, the stories that would impress a crowd at church: someone coming to Christ or getting baptized, mobilizing the whole neighborhood to paint the elderly widow's house, that kind of thing. Now don't get me wrong, those things are great, and they certainly should be celebrated. But those are hardly the only things to celebrate. Remember, anything that anticipates the kingdom of God counts.

One of the most profitable things you can do for your own neighboring is quit paying attention to what your church friends think. Quit letting them decide what is worth celebrating, and return to what Jesus teaches us to celebrate. He taught us to pray "Thy kingdom come, Thy will be done on earth as it is in heaven." Anytime it does, we should celebrate and thank God.

Will you know your neighbors' names in the kingdom of God? Then re-introducing yourself to the lady who lives two houses down and learning her name counts as a success. Praise God for it, and be thankful. Don't feel that you instantly must turn that conversation into an evangelistic encounter. In fact, unless you're one of those rare people who can get away with doing that naturally, please don't. You are better off to move slowly and not spook people than you are to move too fast and scare them away. They live next to you—they aren't going anywhere.

You might have a Christian friend who lays a guilt trip on you because you didn't tell her about Jesus right then. You might have a pastor who wants to know when you're going to invite her to church. *Ignore them.* You can't serve God and seek the praises of men—even Christian leaders—at the same time. No one can serve two masters; don't try. Just do what Jesus said and love your neighbor.

In fact, while we're talking about church, let us recommend that you *not* invite your neighbors to church. Just don't do it. I don't care what your pastor says, building the church *is not your job.* The one and only time in the Bible that Jesus talks about building the church, He says that *He* will do it (Matt 16:18). Trust me, He will do His job. You focus on doing yours: love your neighbors in the name of Jesus. If they don't ever come to church with you, who cares? They are meeting Jesus right in their own neighborhood, *and that is the goal.* Loving your neighbors is your only agenda; don't cloud your mind with church attendance.

The irony is, you probably will end up bringing some neighbors to church with you, at their request—but only if you don't care if they ever come to church. If you have a hidden agenda, they *will* be able to tell, and they won't trust you. So focus on what Jesus said to focus on: loving your neighbor. Trust that He knew what He was doing when He gave us our marching orders.

## Sacramental Neighboring

This doesn't mean that church has nothing to do with how you treat your neighbors. If you understand the lessons God is trying to teach us through the church meeting, then you will have a much deeper understanding of what you are doing with your neighbors, why it works the way it does, and how to do it well. This may be a little hard for you to understand, because the evangelical church has mostly lost its understanding of what is actually going on in a church meeting.

In the end, Christ will return to earth and bring the New Jerusalem down. Heaven will come to earth. But we don't have to wait for the end of history to experience a little bit of heaven. When we gather as believers to worship, we are taken up into heaven. The roof opens, the walls grow thin, and we are in the throne room, the heavenly rnacle, before the throne of God and surrounded by the holy angels and the saints who have gone before us. There, we confess our sins, receive assurance that He has forgiven us, offer up our praises, hear a word from Him, share His Table in peace, and then He sends us into the world as His agents. Heaven is for real—and you go there every Sunday.

When we go out into the world as God's agents, our job is to carry heaven with us, to be walking outposts of the kingdom of God, to anticipate the New Jerusalem everywhere we go. Our lives outside the church gathering are supposed to reflect the heavenly realities that we experience inside the church gathering. In the New Jerusalem, we will feast with Jesus. When we observe the Lord's Table in a church gathering, we are anticipating that future reality in the present.

When you share your food with a friend or a neighbor in your home, you are offering a reflection of the Table, which in turn is a reflection of our future feast in the New Jerusalem. Christ is in you; your neighbor is not just having supper with you; he is having supper with Jesus—"I am with you, even to the end of the age," remember?

Your neighbor doesn't know he's having supper with Jesus. He's not ready to know that yet, so don't tell him; you'll freak him out. But it's true nonetheless, and the reality operates on him—and you—whether he knows it or not. Human beings are built to know that sharing food is a big deal. Traditional cultures have major taboos around whom you eat with and how you can treat someone during a shared meal and often afterward as well. This is because sharing food is sacramental. It reflects realities far larger than we can see.

## Spiritual Exercise #2: Share Food

Your assignment this week is to share food with one neighbor. Don't try to make a production out of it. You don't have to have people over for a full meal. In fact, you don't have to have them into your house at all. You can make a 9x13 pan of brownies and take half of them next door. Say, "I really wanted brownies, and I shouldn't eat all these. Would you like some?"

Before you take the brownies over to your neighbor, take a moment and pray over what you are about to share. Ask God to bless the food and those who eat it, and to use it as a tool to bring His kingdom to your neighborhood. Then go out and share—freely you have received; freely give!

# 2

# Tangible Love: How To Do Basic Neighboring

## Being Present In Your Neighborhood

One of the great diseases of our culture is loneliness and isolation. Our neighborhoods (especially in the suburbs) have been designed to make isolation easy. You can pull in your attached garage after work and walk into your house without ever having to see your neighbors. If you are going to eat or play outdoors, you do it behind the privacy fence in your backyard. You can be in your neighborhood without *really* being present.

So step one in loving your neighbors is often just figuring out how to be present in your particular neighborhood. We've found that people like knowing their neighbors and find their lives enriched when they do. This means if you take the lead on creating a culture of presence in your neighborhood, others are likely to follow suit.

Start spending time in your front yard. If you have kids, put a swing in your front tree and play out there, get some sidewalk chalk.... it'll be fun. Take walks in your neighborhood, greet anyone you see and learn their names. Put a patio set in your front yard and start eating meals out there when the weather is agreeable. Make it a habit of parking on the street and greeting neighbors as you go to your house.

Make time for small talk with your neighbors as you encounter them and always call them by name. If you are mowing the lawn and a neighbor comes home or comes outside, stop the mower and have a chat, and while you're at it, offer them a beer or a lemonade. Relationally, the most valuable thing you have to offer your neighbors is your time and attention. Be present.

## What About Apartments?

People who live in single-family homes have a very different relationship with their neighbors than those of us who live in apartments. As apartment-dwellers, we're usually a pretty transient population, and as with any transient population, we tend not to make friendships based on location. For those of us who have a hard time making friends, someone who might move out next month isn't the best investment of our limited relational capital.

In addition, we literally live on top of each other, and forced proximity takes its toll. As a group, we are much less interested in contact with our neighbors, and much more interested in simply being left alone. It is somewhat awkward to meet a total stranger and discover that this is the same person...

- who you were cursing for playing Katy Perry loudly at midnight.
- whose lovemaking you overheard last night (do you suggest that they move the headboard a little further from the wall, or is that too forward?).
- who is learning violin...and they're *bad* at it.
- who left their laundry in three of the shared dryers for *hours.*
- who always parks so close to the line that the space next to them is nearly unusable.

Our lives already intersect at numerous points, and sometimes it's just easier not to know exactly who is responsible for these things.

There are several problems you have to solve when you live in close proximity with people you don't want to know. The very first is the problem in your own heart. It is easier to have less contact with your neighbors—but God didn't call you to *easy.* God called you to love your neighbors, and He didn't say anything about it being convenient. So commit to overcoming the obstacles.

Your first obstacle is just having contact with people. Depending on the physical setup of your building, that might be quite difficult. Opportunities for contact are coming and going, getting mail, laundry—and that's about it. I once met a guy in the elevator, introduced myself, and discovered that we had been living in the same building for three years together, and our paths had never crossed until that elevator ride. And this is in a small (40-unit) building with only two entrances, one elevator, one set of mailboxes, and one laundry room.

Analyze your environment. Look for the choke points. If you wanted to meet all the people in your building, where would you stand? How can you arrange your personal traffic to maximize your presence in those places? For instance, I live on the 4th floor, and I generally prefer to take the stairs. However, I decided to start taking the elevator *if it gave me a chance to share a ride with someone.* Our elevator is a little slow, so it gives me a chance to have a short conversation. I was surprised to find that mostly, these conversations are positive. I think it's partly because there's a built-in endpoint—the conversation lasts less than 90 seconds, then one of us gets off the elevator.

In fact, because apartment-dwellers are so often averse to contact with their neighbors, you'll need to become a specialist at low-impact, non-threatening contact. Quick conversations, brief contact, small favors. That doesn't mean you can't knock on doors with a plate of brownies—it just means that it won't necessarily get the same kind of reception that it might in a neighborhood of single-family homes.

One possible step toward non-threatening contact is to find another place to meet. In my search for socially acceptable ways to interact with my neighbors, I began to hang out in the little cafe at the end of my block. I encountered some neighbors at this cafe and had better, more meaningful conversations there than I did in our building.

> **Spiritual Exercise #3: Being More Present In Your Neighborhood**
>
> Identify three ways that you could be more present in your neighborhood. It could be as simple as playing with your kids in the front yard instead of the back, or taking an hour to sit in the lobby of your apartment building and read. List them out.
>
> 1. _____
>
> 2. _____
>
> 3. _____
>
> Ask God to help you make a wise choice, then pick one for this week, and do it. If you get around to the other two, that's gravy, but make sure you do at least one of your three, one time this week.
>
> After you do it, celebrate. Thank God for helping you to be more present in your neighborhood. Thank Him even if nothing happened. Thank Him even if it feels like a miserable failure. You are growing in obedience, and that is a success worth celebrating, all by itself. The results are up to God, and He will bring them in His perfect time. Don't worry about getting results you can see—just be faithful.

## Being Present In Your Community Businesses

I got interested in being present to the business owners in my area by accident. I was looking for a neighborhood hangout spot, mostly to meet neighbors and friends. I settled on the cafe at the end of the block, and it turned out (not surprisingly) that the strongest relationships I was able to build were with the owners and workers in the cafe.

Since God was blessing those relationships, I leaned in and began to be conscious about taking a stance of blessing toward these people and their business. I would ask about how business was going, I would pray with them for more customers, I tried to drum up some business through my friends who worked at the hospital across the street, and so on. One particularly rough day, I prayed with the manager, asking God to send customers in the door. When I checked back in with her the next day, she said, "Tim, it was amazing—after you left, people started coming in, and it didn't stop all day!" God wants to bless; sometimes He's just waiting for us to ask. During my time with them, the cafe went through three different owners—the last of whom moved it to a different location. I still go down to see them every now and again, and I continue to pray for God's blessing on their business.

I bias toward small businesses, where one loyal customer can make a noticeable difference. Chains are ok, if the staff is small enough that you can build a relationship with them. Of course, you can't build these relationships for free. During my years at the cafe, I deliberately budgeted extra money to spend there in order to bless them. (And during one bad month, I told the manager that I didn't have any money to spend, but I'd come in and check on her anyway. I did—and that strengthened the relationship even further.)

> **Spiritual Exercise #4**
>
> List ten small businesses close to your home that provide a product or service you can use. Restaurant, coffee shop, pub, hardware store, hobby shop—it doesn't matter what it is, as long as you can be there enough to cultivate relationships.
>
> 1. _____   6. _____
> 2. _____   7. _____
> 3. _____   8. _____
> 4. _____   9. _____
> 5. _____   10. _____
>
> Pick your top three businesses. Write down the names of the staff that you see most often. Pray for them regularly.
>
> 1. _____
> 2. _____
> 3. _____

## Being Available For Opportunities

Presence creates opportunities. If you're in people's lives regularly, there will be significant moments, deep conversations, chances to bless them with actions or words. It isn't up to you when these moments will come. You cannot predict or control them. And I gotta tell you, significant moments have a way of cropping up when you're in a hurry, you have somewhere else to be, when it isn't convenient for you.

You need to mentally prepare for the inconvenience. Determine ahead of time that when God blesses you with opportunities, you will take them. Of course, there will be times when you genuinely do need to go (your daughter just took a bad fall and you're on the way to the ER to find out if her leg is broken), but overall, you need to cultivate a lifestyle of availability. Surrender the idea of being in control and make your peace with being available for the opportunities God gives you.

## Clearing Margin

Margin is the extra space in your life: the time that you have over and above what you need for your regular commitments, the spaces in your schedule that aren't already filled up, the money that isn't going to something already. And it's not just about time, energy and money. There's also relational capacity, headspace, skill sets, spiritual authority, gifting, and so on. But a lot of these other things fall into line if you can clear your schedule a bit.

You can't cultivate a lifestyle of availability if you have no margin. Typical Americans are overscheduled to a ridiculous degree—between work and commuting, church commitments, family responsibilities, extracurricular activities for the kids, hobbies, etc., many of us just have no time at all. You simply can't invest yourself in a ministry of presence until you clear some space.

## Spiritual Exercise #5: Reclaiming Margin In Your Life

Write out your weekly schedule:

|  | Morning | Afternoon | Evening |
|---|---|---|---|
| Sunday |  |  |  |
| Monday |  |  |  |
| Tuesday |  |  |  |
| Wednesday |  |  |  |
| Thursday |  |  |  |
| Friday |  |  |  |
| Saturday |  |  |  |

Pray over your schedule. Ask God to help you discern what you can get rid of or reduce in order to be more available in your neighborhood. Find something you can cut out this week, then reinvest that time in one of the ways of being present that you listed last week in Spiritual Exercise #3.

You will come back to this exercise a number of times over the coming year. As you're able to clear more margin and reinvest those resources in obedience—loving your neighbors as Jesus taught us to do—God will bring kingdom fruit.

## Helping And Asking For Help

Obviously, if you're committing yourself to tangibly loving your literal neighbors, you want to be available to them when they need help. Be willing to help move a refrigerator, fix a fencepost, load or unload a moving truck, babysit, take over a meal, etc. Be alert for opportunities and eager to take them.

Less obvious is the power of asking for help. A lot of people are nervous about taking your help, because they don't want to owe you a favor. (Ask yourself if they have a point. Would *you* want to owe you a favor? If not, you have some work to do on your heart.) Often these same people will be happy for you to owe them a favor. So ask them for help. Quit doing things yourself just because you can manage it alone. Instead ask, "Would it be helpful to have another set of hands?"—and if it would be, then ask someone.

## Coffee And Hangout Time

We have found that simply inviting people into your home for coffee is a great way to connect. People who won't come to your house for a party may be willing to come over for coffee, especially if they feel personally invited and it is not an "event," just a few neighbors getting together for coffee.

There's nothing wrong with creating an event out of a coffee gathering. For a while we did a weekly gathering in our home for coffee on Saturday morning for our neighborhood. It was a great time, and we developed a lot of relationships through it; but in time, interest waned, and we stopped doing it.

My wife and another Christian woman on our block have started a monthly coffee morning for the ladies on the block. This has been very effective; the ladies (most of them retired) not only see this coffee gathering as a tight-knit group of friends, they have also found ways to reach out as a group to bless the neighborhood. Each year they all come together to make a Thanksgiving meal to give to someone in need near our block.

For a while I hosted a pipe and beer night for the guys in the neighborhood. We had some really deep conversations late in the night and prayed together a number of times. The Lord really used that time. Ultimately, after a year or so, we found that the weekly gathering was less effective than the occasional get-together. We still get the guys on the block together for pipes and beers, but only once a month or so.

## Having People Over For Dinner

As far as I know, there is nothing more effective in developing a relationship with someone than having them over for dinner. When you invite a neighbor or a family over for a meal, there is no escaping what is going on. You are sharing your lives over a shared meal.

People eat together, but most people have difficulty having someone over that they don't know all that well. There's more food to be made and more effort expended cleaning up, but that is not where the real difficulty lies. You are inviting someone to be your friend. During the meal, you will sit face-to-face, sharing life with each other. This is sacramental neighboring—you are making a covenant together over bread and wine.

Many of your neighbors are desperate for meaningful relationships and don't realize it. When you invite them over for a meal, you are inviting them into a meaningful relationship. Don't be surprised if they pour out their lives to you. We have found that these times can be exhausting, and consequently, we don't do it often. But when we do, amazing things happen; in general after a shared meal, you never go back to the way things were before. You are friends.

## A Neighborhood Event

When the New Jerusalem descends to earth and God dwells among us, we will all come to know each other. So blessing your neighborhood doesn't stop with you meeting your neighbors and being kind to them. It also means helping them to meet each other and build strong relationships. A lot of that work can be done two or three people at a time, over a cup of coffee, around a fire pit in the evening, or in a chance meeting on the sidewalk. But there's a place for a neighborhood event that gives a large group of people an opportunity to mix with each other.

We're going to lay out three options for such an event, ranging from as easy as possible to pretty labor-intensive.

- **"Happy Hour"** - everybody brings their brown bag lunch/supper for a picnic on your front lawn. You don't supply any of the food, you just invite people over. Maybe

you supply soda and lemonade, if you want.
- **Neighborhood Barbecue** - A grilling event that you host. You supply condiments, paper products, and the grill (and maybe borrow a few from the neighbors). You tell the neighbors to bring their own meat to grill, and bring a side to share.
- **Block Party** - A big shindig worth closing down the street for. You might supply a rented bouncy castle, a cotton candy machine, and burgers. You're going to need a lot of cooperation to pull this off, so think twice about it unless you already have good relationships with your neighbors.

For any neighborhood event, spreading the word is key, and the bigger the event, the more time you'll need to talk it up. Start by feeling people out. Casually mention that you had the idea to do the event, and see what kind of reactions you get. You are looking for "people of peace" (Luke 10:6) who might be receptive to the idea and willing to help it succeed. You are also listening for other ideas—once you start the conversation about a neighborhood event, don't be surprised if one of your neighbors has better ideas than you do!

When you have a few allies (or at least a few people who aren't opposed to the idea), you can move to the next stage. Set a date, and start spreading the word. If you can get away with it, ask some people for help. If they commit to help you, they'll probably show up (if they actually help, that's a bonus, but be happy if

## HAPPY HOUR CHECKLIST

People I am going to mention my idea to:
_____

My allies are/people whom I can ask to help:
_____

Is there someone who will be offended if I forget to invite them?
_____

I will make a special effort to invite:
_____
_____

The week before, I will spread the word through the neighborhood by:
_____
_____

What meal will I make for my family? (We recommend something simple, so you can save your energy for hosting.
_____

Am I going to provide drinks? If so, what am I going to provide and how am I going to do it? (We recommend 2-liter bottles, red cups, and a couple bags of ice—easy and cheap.)
_____

Am I going to provide music? (You need a playlist that will be fun, light, and *not* churchy. If you don't think you can pull that off, consider playing a local radio station.)
_____

Where will I set up lawn chairs, tables, and/or picnic blankets?
_____

## NEIGHBORHOOD BARBECUE CHECKLIST

People I am going to mention my idea to:

_____

My allies are/people whom I can ask to help:

_____

Is there someone who will be offended if I forget to invite them?

_____

I will make a special effort to invite:

_____

_____

The week before, I will spread the word through the neighborhood by:

_____

Supplies I need to provide…(paper products, plasticware, serving utensils, large trash can, lawn chairs and tables, large table for people's side dishes, grill and full propane tank/plenty of charcoal, cooler for drinks)

_____

Food I need to provide…(condiments, a side dish, meat to grill for my family and some extra meat for others)

_____

Drinks I'm going to provide…(a large cooler of ice and water bottles, soda cans, and juice boxes; or 2-liter bottles, red cups, and a couple bags of ice)

_____

Games/activities I will provide or ask a neighbor to bring…(this one's not necessary, and you don't need to go overboard, but a few simple things can add a lot: sidewalk chalk, bubbles for young kids, lawn bowling, etc.)

_____

## BLOCK PARTY CHECKLIST

People I am going to mention my idea to:
_____

My allies are/people whom I can ask to help:
_____

Is there someone who will be offended if I forget to invite them?
_____

I will make a special effort to invite:
_____
_____

If we're planning to shut down the street....
    (1)...have we talked to *every* household that will be affected by the shut-down?
    (2)...have we talked to the local authorities to see if we can do that?

The week before, I will spread the word through the neighborhood by...(we recommend fliers or door-hangers for a 2-to 3-block radius)
_____
_____

Supplies I need to provide...(paper products, plasticware, serving utensils, large trash cans, lawn chairs and tables, large tables for people's food dishes, grills and full propane tanks/plenty of charcoal, coolers, balloons and decorations)
_____
_____

continued on next page....

Food I need to provide...(burgers and buns, condiments, side dishes, desserts)

_____

_____

Drinks I'm going to provide...(large coolers of ice and water bottles, soda cans, and juice boxes)

_____

Games/activities I will provide or ask a neighbor to bring...(bouncy castle, outdoor games such as lawn bowling, croquet, badminton, speakers for music, live musicians, etc.)

_____

_____

### Spiritual Exercise #6: A Neighborhood Event

If you're not quite ready to do an event in your own neighborhood, then help someone else do one in their neighborhood and get a feel for what it might be like.

You can do a "happy hour" type event just because, but certain times of the year are more conducive to big events: Christmas time, Halloween, New Year's, July 4th, the first warm weather of summer. (Thanksgiving not so much—it tends to be a family day.)

Remember, assume a stance of blessing. You're not there to get people to church or even to tell them about Jesus—not this time. You're there to *show* them the love of Jesus.

they just show up). Recruit enough helpers, and your event is guaranteed to be a success. Even for a "happy hour" type event where you're not really providing anything, you can ask your allies to bring extra lawn chairs so people will have places to sit.

If you are providing anything, make lists and make your grocery runs at least a day before. Overbuy—you can use or give away the excess, but you don't want to run out.

The morning of the event, start making some visible preparations. Drag the grill around into the front yard, put out some lawn chairs, whatever you can do to make it obvious at a glance that SOMETHING IS GOING TO HAPPEN HERE TODAY.

## Rolling With The Punches

Things don't always work out the way you might have imagined. I started a weekly coffee morning hoping that it would continue for years and foster relationships through our neighborhood. But it didn't work out that way. It was a good vehicle for a time; then we found that we could be more effective if we put energy elsewhere. So we did.

The goal is to love your neighbors. If a particular vehicle accomplishes that now, great. If it stops working, stop using it and find something else. Just because some vehicle doesn't work in developing relationships doesn't mean you have failed. Pray, trust God, and try something different.

## Long-Term Strategy In Practice

You will find that some neighbors are resistant to your efforts to develop a relationship with them. They may avoid you or cut your conversations short. That doesn't excuse you from loving them, but there's also not too much you can do about it *right now*. That's okay; you are in it for the long term.

There is only one couple on our block at our same stage of life. They live nearby, are about our age, race, and socioeconomic status. They have been friendly when we've reached out to them, but have not seemed interested in getting to know us. For a while, this was discouraging, but we're in it for the long haul. So we keep praying for them, asking God to show us when and how to connect to them.

Several months ago, I told my wife that if/when this couple started having children, that would present some opportunities. Shortly thereafter, we found out that they were expecting. Maybe that will open a door. Maybe not. In the meantime, we wait and trust God to provide that opportunity.

A lot of neighborhood ministry is like that. Things you think will be great opportunities don't turn out that way. Unlikely opportunities blossom overnight. Don't get discouraged. Don't hurry. God is in control, and for the most part, these people aren't going anywhere. You can afford to be patient, and just look for opportunities as they arise.

# 3

## Growing in Love: Spiritual Friendship and Leadership

Remember Jesus' lesson: when you go to a dinner party, don't grab the best seat. Take a lowly place, and wait to be invited to the seat of honor. If you tangibly love your actual neighbors, you will unavoidably find yourself in a place of influence. Don't rush it, and don't grab for it. You don't need to. God is preparing you for the place of influence He wants you to have, and He is preparing your neighbors to receive you. He will give you their hearts in His timing.

You may be surprised by who God gives you. The neighbor that asked you where you go to church the second week and seemed wide-open may take a long time. The hopeless pothead in the run-down rental house down the street may come into your sphere of influence a lot faster.

There's another side effect of tangibly loving your neighbors that we need to mention to you. When your neighbors begin to give to you, *don't* turn down the gifts. God built a sacramental reality into human nature: we tithe back to the people who minister God's image to us. This was enshrined into law in ancient Israel, where all the other tribes tithed to the Levites who lived among them. But you can see it even in the poorest communities and roughest biker gangs today, which take care of their best mechanics and musicians, because those people provide for the rest of the group. As you become effective at tangibly loving your neighbors and being the image of God in your community, they will naturally begin to "tithe" back to you.

When we moved into our neighborhood we naturally filled a void; no one was connecting the neighbors with each other or providing a context for community life to take place. We were surprised that many of the people on our block had never met even though they had lived just a couple houses down from each other for years. We connected many of these neighbors to each other through parties and coffee mornings, and they actually liked one another! Then something interesting happened: they started doing things for us. Two neighbors would regularly shovel our sidewalks in the winter. Another neighbor would bring us produce from her garden. One neighbor gave us a bunch of small kitchen appliances that were still new in their packaging (she had bought them for herself, but never ended up using them). At a party recently, a number of neighbors who didn't attend the party dropped by to give us food for the potluck. At first when these things started to happen, we couldn't make sense of it, but we realized that people felt a sense of obligation to us for our leadership on the block and were, in a sense, tithing to us.

## Low-Impact Habits

Our goal here is to give you some simple things you can do that will help you begin to operate as a spiritual influence in your neighborhood.

The first and most obvious thing is praying with your neighbors. The opportunities are everywhere, and it's only weird if you make it weird. You're taking a walk and run into a neighbor. You say "Hi, how are you?" and in the minute or so of casual conversation, she tells you that she has a bad headache. It is as simple as this:

You: "Would it be all right if I prayed for your headache?"

Her: "Uh...I guess so."

You: "Lord God, Jane has a nasty headache, and I know she's got stuff to do today. Please make the headache go away so she can have an enjoyable day."

It doesn't have to be any more complicated than that. When you ask if you can pray for her, Jane doesn't necessarily think that you are going to do it right then—but you can get away with it if you keep it to one or two sentences and you don't get all religious about it. The theology you need to know here is simple: Jesus' last words to us before He left, *literally* His last words, were "I am with you always, even to the end of the age (Matt 28:20)." He is here. He is standing at your shoulder, the third person in the conversation. So when you pray, speak to Him as though He is right there, *because He is*. Don't use a ton of religious language, and for heaven's sake don't go into "prayer mode" like you're in church. Just talk.

He's a real person and He's right there. What better way for Jane to discover Jesus?

It doesn't matter whether it's a headache, an unexpected pregnancy, a late mortgage payment, the mother-in-law coming for a visit, a kid going to preschool for the first time—or college—whatever the concern might be, take it to God. Present it to Him.

You do this because God cares, and He wants to hear from you. Your neighbor may not believe that, and that's okay. You believe it enough for both of you, which is what "sharing your faith" *really* means.

"But what if God doesn't answer the prayer?" A lot of people ask us this, and it's a good question. There are three answers to it, all of them important for your spiritual growth.

The first answer is that we ask because Jesus told us to. He taught us to pray, "Thy kingdom come, Thy will be done on earth as it is in heaven." We know a little about what the kingdom of God will ultimately look like, when the New Jerusalem descends to earth and God dwells with His people: no more pain, sickness, or grief. So it is always appropriate to ask for God's kingdom to come on earth as it is in heaven. We can always ask God to relieve pain, heal the sick, comfort the grieving, restore broken relationships, and so on. God may not respond in exactly the way we are hoping when we ask—but that's His business. Let God worry about His reputation; we need to be concerned with obedience. He said to ask for these things—let's ask.

Obedience is a sufficient answer to the question, but there's more to say here. The second answer to "What if God doesn't answer the prayer?" is to examine your own heart. Perhaps you are reluctant to ask God to relieve your neighbor's headache because *you don't think He'll really do it*. Perhaps you have little experience with God answering prayers of this kind—but the Bible tells us that we do not have because we do not ask. Could it be that God is ready to answer these requests, if only we would ask for them? Why don't we trust Him and find out?

The third answer is based in our experience of praying for our neighbors. In our experience, we have not seen anyone alienated from God because He didn't take away their headache. Maybe it's happened with somebody somewhere, but it's not something to worry about. Rather, we see our neighbors touched that we are willing to pray for them, *regardless of the outcome*. Sometimes God answers prayer by giving us exactly what we asked for, bringing His kingdom to earth right in front of us. Sometimes He doesn't—but we have to remember that it's *His* kingdom, not ours. He is entitled to do things His way. In our experience, when God chooses not to give us what we ask, He does it in a way that doesn't hurt His reputation. And that is exactly what we should expect when we live a life of obedience.

In the same way that you pray for your neighbors' concerns, you can easily speak blessing over your neighbors. You may have to work up to it—Christians have lost the art of speaking blessing even over each other, much less over unbelievers. But this is pretty simple. Blessing is calling on God to do something good. So you're talking with Dave, a contractor who lives across the street, and he mentions that he's starting a new project this week. "May God bless you with a safe and profitable job." That's all you have to say. Think you can do that?

Yes, you can. Practice on your Christian friends first if you have to, but build the habit. Get comfortable with it. It's only weird if you make it weird.

> **Spiritual Exercise #7: Blessing/Praying with a Neighbor**
>
> Just do it. Next time you're talking with a neighbor, if the conversation involves *anything* more than the weather, if they let slip any detail of what they're up to that day, or some obstacle they're facing—basically anything happening in their life that God could help them with—then say a blessing or pray with them. Blessing is easier—"May God bless you with a great birthday party for your daughter this afternoon."
>
> This is actually really easy if you don't let yourself overthink it. So just go do it.

## Warfare

*Praying for your Neighborhood*
As you learn the names of your neighbors, pray for them by name as a family. Find a way to divide them up so that you pray for all your neighbors every week. If you have important events coming up in the neighborhood—a birth, a move, the anniversary of a marriage, a death, a divorce—pray for them too.

*Claiming your Block*
Another important step you can take toward the kingdom of God is to claim your block or your street. Gather your friends and family and take a walk up and down your street, praying for the families that live

there and asking God to bring His kingdom to each house. At the ends of the street or the corners of the block, pray and claim the block for Jesus Christ and His kingdom, and ask God to give you the territory. Do you believe that God will give you your block? Maybe not—but maybe He hasn't because you never asked. Ask, and see what He will do.

Be aware that this is real warfare. Once you claim the ground, you're going to have to fight for it, and whatever ground you take, you're going to have to hold against an enemy intent on taking it back. Be prepared to spend time in prayer regularly for your block and for your family.

*House Blessings*

Doing a house blessing is pretty simple in concept, however daunting it may sound. For a full house blessing, the goal is very simple: when you leave, there should be no place in the home left unblessed, no one who lives there who has not been prayed for, no legitimate activity that you have not asked God to make fruitful. Does it make a difference? Well, do you believe God answers prayer?

We're not going to try to convince you that you should go out and do house blessings. If you want to blow it off and skip to the next section, you go right ahead. Here's what's going to happen: if you make a habit of praying for and blessing your neighbors, it won't be very long before someone comes to you and says, "There's this room in my house that just feels wrong. It always has. It's like something bad happened there, and it's still hanging in the air. Will you come and pray over my house?" When that happens, however much it might scare you or just seem weird, you're going to feel like you have to say yes. You might just pray over that room, or you might do a full house blessing, but you won't feel right telling your neighbor that you won't come and pray for their house.

So if this section seems silly now, go ahead and skip it. It'll be here when you need it. If you need a little Bible to undergird this, here are some verses that might help. Jesus told His disciples to heal the sick, cast out demons, and proclaim the good news (Matt 10:8). If there's a demon in someone's house, and they want you to kick it out, well...are you following Jesus or not? Leviticus 14:33-53 describes the priest's role in cleansing a leprous house under the Old Covenant. As a minister of the New Covenant, how much more willing should you be to cleanse a home from spiritual contagion, to bless and dedicate it?

So since you're going to end up doing this even if it scares you or you think it's silly, let's talk about how to go about it. The basic idea is that you're going to bless the home and its occupants as extensively as you can. Go through the home and bless every room and the activities that take place there. Pray over the doors, for people of peace to enter. Pray for good conversation and the growth of deep friendships in the dining room. Pray for safety and productivity in the workshop. If it's a single-family home with a yard, you might go out to the four corners of the property and dedicate the whole property to God's kingdom and His purposes. And so on (we'll have more suggestions for you later).

This is a significant act of spiritual authority, so take a small team with you if you can. There's nothing wrong with just going by yourself if you have to—better that than not doing it at all—but it's best if you can bring a mix of men and women and a mix of spiritual gifts. Different people process things differently and see different needs, so bring the wisdom and strength of the Body to bear.

Here's how we typically do it. We'll gather the team somewhere away from the house we're going to bless—one of the team members' homes, usually—and spend some time checking in with each other, praying for each other and for the work we're going to do. Then we go together to the home we're going to bless. We prefer that everyone who lives there be present, but if somebody's not home, that won't stop us from praying for them in their absence.

Once we're in the home, we'll introduce everyone, and ask the family if they have any particular requests or information about the home or family that they think we should know. There will often be something: "Could you pray over the garage? I always feel unsafe out there." Usually further information will surface as we go as well. Then we'll lay out a plan and get to work.

As far as the physical layout goes, we usually work from the outside in, starting from the corners of the property and then working our way through the house. There's nothing magical about that way of doing it—it's just an order that makes sense, and flows well. The whole team and the family will go together to each place and pray over it. Some of the requests will be literal, like praying at the front door for visitors to enter with good intentions. Other requests might be more metaphorical, like praying in the bathrooms for spiritual as well as physical

> **Prepping a Family for House Blessing**
>
> Explain that there's nothing magical about praying over a house. God answers prayer, and He responds to His people speaking blessing. That's enough explanation for most people. If you feel the need, you might also explain that you may pray against any demonic attachments that may be there. Be sure to explain that demonic attachments don't mean that they are bad people or they've done something wrong; it just means they're being attacked. Demons certainly do attack deliberate sin, but they also seek to exploit fear, depression, sadness, illness, others' sins against us, and all kinds of things that aren't our fault. Dealing with a demon just means that the demon saw an opportunity to attack—we're not here to judge anybody.
>
> That said, also explain that if the demon has come because there is deliberate sin, then continued deliberate sin will open a door for the demon to come back. So If you're casting out an unclean spirit and they suddenly realize why it's there, that is a good time to confess the sin and renounce it.

cleanliness. Look for the relevant analogies and use them.

Some things you might pray for:
- Front yard
  - good interactions with neighbors
  - safe play for the kids
- Back yard
  - safe play for the kids
  - family bonding
- Front door

- for those who enter to experience the peace of Christ
- for God to protect the family from those who might enter with bad intentions
- Living room/den
  - good family bonding
  - enjoyable playtimes
  - good conversations with friends and neighbors
- Kitchen
  - abundant provision for the family
  - enough to share with neighbors and friends
- Bedrooms
  - restful sleep
  - ask God to take away nightmares (if anyone's having them)
  - for God to speak to them in their dreams
  - God's blessing on their lovemaking (if appropriate)
  - for more children (if appropriate)
  - if you happen to know that "monsters under the bed" (and in the closet, and so forth) are an issue for one of the children, take the time to pray about it. (Otherwise, don't bring it up—you don't want to create a problem where there isn't one.) Sometimes these are just fruits of overactive imagination, but sometimes they are not, and many parents don't know what to do with a child who sees things they can't.

- Bathrooms
    - physical cleanliness and health
    - for those who look in the mirror to see themselves as God sees them
    - for beauty of the spirit as well as outward beauty
- Laundry areas
    - for God to infuse the necessary housekeeping tasks with joy
    - for God to give the family the resources to deal with their "dirty laundry"
- Garage/storage areas
    - for the family possessions to be preserved against water leaks, pests, etc.
    - for a healthy flow of possessions in and out of the family
    - safe shelter for the family vehicle(s) and safe travel in it
- Workshop/hobby room
    - for time to invest in hobbies
    - for the opportunity to disengage from daily work and rest by doing something fun
    - for the home to stay in good repair
- Home office
    - good work/life balance
    - for really productive work when it's time to work
    - for the strength to set work aside when it's time to be with the family

Rotate through your team, letting different people pray as they feel led. If someone feels like more prayer is needed in a particular place, or if there's something specific to pray for/against in a particular place, then by all means, do that. Often further information will surface as you move room to room. "This used to be Uncle Bobby's room. He killed himself in here back in '82." As these things surface, pray for them specifically. Without condemnation, confess whatever sins need to be confessed as sins, renounce them in Jesus' name, and break any spiritual attachments that have come about as a result of them. That might look like this:

"Lord God, we aren't here to condemn Uncle Bobby. We know he was in a lot of pain, and we don't know everything that was in his heart when he decided to kill himself. We know that You saw his heart, and we trust You to sort all that out. But we also know that life and death are Yours to give, and it isn't right to take those things into our own hands. So we confess to You that Uncle Bobby made the wrong decision. We renounce suicide in Jesus' name, and in Jesus' name we cast out any unclean spirits that have come here as a result of Uncle Bobby's decision.

[To the spirits] You must leave, in Jesus' name. You are no longer welcome here.

[To God] Lord God, we ask You to send Your Holy Spirit to fill this place with Your presence and to fill the people who spend time in this room with His fruit. Specifically, we ask for this room to become a place of joy, peace, and hope rather than a place of despair. In Jesus name, Amen."

After you pray your way through the house, you might also pray over each of the occupants of the house. If you have prophetically gifted team members, use them—but be sure they understand that this is a house *blessing*, not a time to run riot. If they are

## The Appropriate Use of the Prophetic Gifts

1 Corinthians 14:3 says, "He who prophesies speaks edification, exhortation and comfort." In other words, build up, lift up, and cheer up. This is the use to which your prophetic gifts should be put. So let's say you are praying over the husband's home office, and you get a sudden strong surge of lust or an image of him looking at pornography at his computer. Do not yell "STOP LOOKING AT PORN IN HERE!" thereby embarrassing the man in front his family and your team. Good luck having a chance to love your neighbor after that.

Calling him out that way is not going to be a blessing, and that's what you've been invited into the home for. So if you can't find a way to use that information to build up, lift up, or cheer up, then just keep your trap shut and take it as a call to (silently) hold him up in prayer. But often a better option is to take the information that God has given you and deliver a word that builds up, lifts up, and cheers up. Thus: "Lord God, I ask you to bless Bob with focus as he works. Make his time here productive, and help him not to linger here when the work is done. Help him to know that he's done everything productive that he can for the day, and go be with his family." Or you could wait until the end when you're praying over him and say "Bob, I feel very strongly that God is calling you to a new level of purity and devotion to your wife," and then pray for that. Some prophetically gifted people balk at the idea that it is their job to bless and encourage rather than to call out sin in a hellfire-and-damnation way. Do not bring these people with you on a house blessing.

> **Spiritual Exercise #8: Neighborhood Warfare**
>
> We have laid out a few possibilities for neighborhood spiritual warfare: Praying for your neighborhood, claiming your block, and house blessings. Pick something from that list and do it.
>
> Afterwards, take a moment to sit down and debrief. What went well? Thank God for it. What will you do differently next time? Thank God for the lesson. Whatever happened, thank God.
>
> Then go out and do some more.

unable to rise to the occasion and take a definite stance of blessing, leave them at home.

When you're done going through the house, don't just disperse from there. Take the team back to where you started and debrief. Take some time to discuss what you just went through—impressions, thoughts, successes to celebrate, mistakes to avoid next time. Pray with and for each other, and ask God to protect each other from spiritual blowback—which is common when you do this kind of work. When you push the darkness, the darkness pushes back.

Don't underestimate this kind of work. It is real warfare; it is very significant, and the enemy will treat it that way. In the days following a house blessing, it is common to come under significant spiritual attack. Don't be afraid of this—just understand that it's warfare, and fight back.

## Pastoral Ministry In Your Neighborhood

If you become the sort of person who prays for and with your neighbors, who speaks blessing over them, who prays earnestly for the Kingdom to come on your block, then you will be asked to do more, because that's how the Kingdom works. "To the one who has, more will be given (Mark 4:25)." When someone's mother is in the hospital, they will ask you to come visit. They won't ask for your pastor; they will ask for *you*. Don't you dare shirk your responsibility. Go. You don't have to do anything different than what you've been doing all along. What you've been doing all along—praying and blessing—is why they are asking for you. So go. Listen. Love. Pray and bless.

Of course, you can't do everything, and sometimes the demands of the situation will exceed your skills. The couple across the street might ask if you know someone who can marry them. That neighbor two doors down that you've never, ever seen sober? Maybe she does need to be in a program. So do what a good friend does. A good friend doesn't try to solve all the problems; a good friend connects people to resources and then stays connected to the process. Call your pastor for the couple across the street, but check back in with them to see how it's going. When the lady two doors down is ready to get sober, drive her to a meeting, and stand by her while she walks through the process.

Jesus is in your neighborhood—He is always with you. Some of the things that happen in your neighborhood will be beyond your resources, but none of them will be beyond Him. Stay connected and trust Him to work.

# Occasional Articles

These articles chronicle some of our early attempts to cast vision for neighborhood ministry, taking a stance of blessing, building kingdom culture, and related topics. They're not as tightly integrated as the primer you just read, but they address a kaleidoscope of issues that will give you some other vantage points from which to think about loving your neighbors. If you find them helpful, stay tuned at headwatersresources.org for further installments.

# Neighborhood Culture Articles

*In the New Jerusalem, when the kingdom of God is fully realized, we will know and love our neighbors. These articles are our meditations on what it might look like to anticipate that culture in our neighborhoods right now.*

## Neighborhood Ministry

November 20, 2012

*Thy Kingdom come...one block at a time.*

Remember on old sitcoms when a mom would send her son to the neighbor's house to borrow an egg or a cup of flour? That actually used to happen, and it wasn't too long ago. Now a person can live in an apartment or house and not even meet their next-door neighbors for years — *and everybody thinks that this is completely normal.*

As a result of this isolation, people are starving for community and they often don't even know it. Instead of taking part in actual interaction, they are filling that hole with a variety of substitutes and idols. Some of the things they fill the hole with are good: sports, church activities, concerts. The problem is, these things that they do with friends scattered all over the city have a way of crowding out anything they might do with the people who live next door.

Confronted by the incongruity of this situation, the most natural thing in the world is to defend what we're already doing. Of course, we should love our neighbors as ourselves — it's the second greatest commandment. But we are already investing in people who share common interests with us, and we naturally spend time with them. Sure, we probably don't love them as well as we should, but maybe we should invest more in *those* natural relationships instead of trying to bridge the gap to the total stranger next door. After all, isn't there more than one way to define "neighbor?"

And there it is. "Who is my neighbor?"

As Christians, we should be suspicious when we catch ourselves asking that question. Jesus once told the parable of the Good Samaritan to address that very point, and the gist of it is that everybody is your neighbor. But we now live in a time when people act as though they have "neighbors" far away, but the guy next door is somehow *not* their neighbor. This is strange. This is not the way the world should be.

The strangeness of our world presents an incredible opportunity for Christians to bring the kingdom to their neighborhoods. But how? Practically speaking, we just don't have the time to get to know each of our neighbors. The kids have soccer practice three nights a week; and we need to take care of our marriage, so that's one date night a week; then there's youth group, meetings...on and on. Part of the answer to this is simply, "Make room for it!" After all, we *are* talking about the second greatest commandment. But there's more to it than that. How can we reach our neighbors effectively in a way that doesn't burn us out?

Headwaters is currently in the early stages of experimenting with ways of reaching our neighbors. We take it on faith that there is a way to obey God's command to love our neighbors while maintaining proper priorities, resting well, and not burning out — we just have to find it.

Through our early experiments, we have hit on an approach that works for us, and we think it might work for you, too. We aren't saying this is the only way God can reach a neighborhood, but this is what He seems to be blessing in our setting. Below are a few of the key points. Some of them are a bit provocative, but we will have posts on each point in the coming weeks explaining further and showing why it is an essential part of our approach.

Neighborhood outreach must happen within the context of a core Christian community.

That community *cannot* be a church.

That community *must* have representatives from multiple churches.

The ministry focus must be geographical, not interest- or demographically-based.

## Parish Community: Why You Need a Team to Reach Your Neighborhood

*(Back in 2012, we were experimenting with a different language, trying to find the right way to talk about this whole "loving your neighbor" thing in a way that gave people a vision for what could happen. "Parish Community" was one of the early experiments. It was an attempt to highlight the possibility of spiritual leadership in your neighborhood, working collaboratively with, but also independently of, your local churches.)*

December 13, 2012

*Thy Kingdom come...one block at a time.*

In John 17 Jesus prays for us: "that all of them may be one, Father, just as you are in me and I am in you. May they also be in us so that the world may believe that you have sent me." When the world sees Christians living in unity, they believe in Jesus. According to Jesus, this is the normal way that unbelievers come to the Lord.

When we talk about evangelism, we usually mean *telling people about Christ*. The method of evangelism that comes out of John 17:20-21 is one where we *show them Christ in community*. Have you noticed that this doesn't happen that often in our culture? People regularly come to Christ by seeing the faithfulness of a friend who knows the Lord, or the compassion shown them by a Christian friend, but rarely do you hear about an unbeliever who came to Christ because he saw Christ in Christians who truly love one another.

One reason that unbelievers don't come to Christ this way is because they've never seen Christians loving one another in community. After all, where would they go to see it? If they go to church, they sit in the audience and see a show far more than they see a community in action.

Jesus' prayer in John 17 is the basis for our neighborhood outreach: we want to invite our neighbors into Christian community so that they might believe in Jesus. In our last post on reaching your neighborhood, we made the point that people are increasingly isolated from their next-door neighbors and are consequently starving for community, so we are offering something that meets a cultural need.

Practically, this means hosting monthly parties where we invite our neighbors to experience Christian community.

How do we make that happen? Imagine a nice Christian couple buys their first house, and after settling in, invites every neighbor on the block over for food and drink. Suppose the Lord gives them favor with their neighbors and 35 people come over, including the other Christian couple that lives on the block. The party is a blast, live music, a great meal and a few beers. Great. But what makes this any different than the local bar? Sure you have some Christians there, and maybe Jesus is mentioned in a couple of conversations; but what you have is an unbelieving community with a couple of Christians in attendance, *not* a Christian community.

In order to show our neighbors a John 17 Christian community, we have to have enough Christians at the gathering to establish the cultural center of gravity. That means we need a significant number of Christians who know each other and are already living as a community. Two Christian couples just isn't enough; if you have, say, 28 Christians at party where there are 50 total people, now you have a Christian community.

Of course, you'll probably have a hard time locating 28 Christians on your block, so gathering the necessary people will be your first major logistical problem. The logistics of pulling this together will be the subject of our next neighborhood ministry post.

## The Logistics of Parish Community

January 1, 2013

*Thy Kingdom come...one block at a time.*
As we discussed in the last post, the goal of a parish community is to invite your neighbors into a place where they can see Christian community in action the way Jesus prayed in John 17.

Here's the problem: If you live on a block with 20 houses, chances are there is one other Christian family; hardly enough to establish a Christian community on your block alone. If you live in the suburbs, the percentage of Christians is going to be a bit higher. If you live in an apartment, it will be a bit lower. But in any case, unless you live in a *very* uncommon neighborhood, you simply don't have enough Christian neighbors to establish the cultural center of gravity. You cannot invite your neighbors into a Christian community right in their own neighborhood if you haven't got enough Christians to do it. So where are you going to get the necessary people?

What we want your neighbors to see is a community of people living out John 17. So let's look at John 17 — what does it say? Jesus prays that His people will be one. He says nothing about church or denominational boundaries; He just wants His people to be one. So cast the net a little wider than a few blocks — say, a two-mile radius around where you live. Draw your Christians from there. Go ahead and cross church and denominational lines. There are a lot of good reasons to do that, but for now, just think about it as a matter of obedience and practical necessity. If you want 25 local Christians, and the closer the better, it behooves you to quit worrying about what church they go to and just invite whoever God has planted around you.

Having a team — what we are calling a parish community — also makes this sustainable. Hosting a house full of people is a *lot* of work. If you have to do all the set up, all the food prep and all the clean up every time, you aren't going to do it very often. It's just not going to happen. But suppose you don't have to worry about the food at all. One of your team members is coordinating food, and you have 25 Christians each bringing a dish, a drink, or a dessert. You have one couple that will come early to help set up, and two more couples who have volunteered to stay late and clean up afterward. Suddenly, hosting the party gets a lot simpler.

## Why Your Parish Community Can't All Come From The Same Church

*January 5, 2013 by Tim Nichols*

*Thy Kingdom come...one block at a time.*
Once you understand the need for a core Christian community — we're calling it a "parish community" — in order to reach your neighborhood, the temptation is to just recruit a handful of families from your church to come reach your block for Christ. You should resist this temptation.

Have you ever been to a social gathering where gradually, over the course of the evening, it became clearer and clearer that all these people were somehow connected to each other? Maybe there seemed to be four or five families present, but they all turned out to be cousins. Maybe it turned out that they all worked at the same place. Maybe they were all involved in selling Amway products...and they were recruiting! Remember how the sense of weirdness gradually increased until the "aha!" moment when it all became clear how they were connected to each other?

Now imagine this happening at your neighborhood gathering. A half-dozen of your neighbors are there, and then, halfway through the evening, one of them realizes that all the people who *don't* live on the block go to church together — all 25 of them. And nobody mentioned it. How do you think that's going to go over? Your neighbors are going to be weirded out. We don't want them to feel like there's some undercover church membership drive going on, *because there isn't!* We aren't trying to get our neighbors to come to church — not our church, not any church. It's just not about that.

Let's take it a step further. Suppose a Christian family from down the block comes to your neighborhood gathering, but they go to a different church in town. Now this family may be the only other Christian family on your whole block. Thinking geographically, they ought to be your closest allies; after all, you can see their house from your front porch, and "a neighbor nearby is better than a brother far away" (Prov 27:10). But because you have chosen to draw your whole parish community from your church, the Christian family from your own street starts out as an outsider. Depending on the culture of your church group, they may never be able to become a part of that core community, and in that case you have created the very problem you are trying to avoid. Rather than inviting your unbelieving neighbors into a John 17 community, you are inviting them into a culture where believers are divided from each other by church affiliation.

Now maybe the culture of your church is such that you can overcome this and welcome in believers from other churches. (Most people think their church is that welcoming. Usually, they are wrong — but let's say your church is the exception.) The question is, why create the problem in the first place when you can avoid it altogether? Why not begin by drawing believers from multiple churches into your parish community?

We simply want to show our neighbors a little slice of the Kingdom of God in action — God's people loving one another in the way that Jesus prayed we would in John 17. While a single church community can certainly show John 17 to a limited extent, the thing really comes into its own when you have Christians from a number of different churches drawing together to love one another *simply because they're Christian neighbors*. They don't go to the same church or share the same hobby; what they have in common is Jesus, and that's enough. When this happens, the Kingdom of God is coming into the neighborhood: neighbors are loving and caring for one another.

That neighborhood love and care is what we want, so *that is what we are modeling.* Our core group contains Christians from at least four different local churches, and there are probably seven to nine churches represented at any given large gathering. What do we all have in common? We are followers of

Jesus who live in Englewood, mostly within about a mile of the home where we're gathering. We're there to meet our neighbors, to get to know them, and to love them. That's all, and that's enough.

## Parish Community: How Service Fits In

*January 9, 2013*

*Thy Kingdom come...one block at a time.*
In our first post on reaching neighborhoods we shared how people are increasingly isolated from their neighbors and are therefore starving for community. So when we talk about Headwaters' approach to serving our neighbors, that hunger is where we start.

We know that there are a number of immediate practical needs in our neighborhood: perhaps the widow on the corner needs her gutters cleaned out and the family with four kids needs some financial help getting the minivan fixed. These are important, but *we don't start with service projects, because we can't*. Right now we don't even know these people well enough to really understand their needs, and even if we knew all of their needs, there's no sustainable way we could handle the load by ourselves. We haven't got the time, money, and energy.

With the resources of a big church behind us, we could do some of these things up front, but we don't have that. Even if we did, we're doing long-term work with the people we live next to, not a quick community-service experience for the high school youth group. The church would have to be committed to the neighborhood for the long haul, and most churches simply aren't prepared to do that.

Of course, we *could* go spend a Saturday morning cleaning out gutters, and there would be nothing wrong with doing that. If a pressing need comes to our attention, we will. We look forward to being able to serve in ways that will advance the Kingdom. That last bit is key. We're after more than just a quick community service fix; we want to see the Kingdom of God.

What will meeting the community's needs look like in the Kingdom of God? In the Kingdom where lion and lamb lie down together, and the young child plays by the cobra's hole, there won't be one family on the block taking care of everyone else; *we will all care for each other.*

So we start by creating community, establishing a context in which needs can be met *by the community.* Cleaning out gutters is a great start, but it's the very least of it. We want *all* the things that happened where Jesus walked to happen in our neighborhood: "The blind receive sight, the lame walk, those who have leprosy are cured, the deaf hear, the dead are raised, and the good news is preached to the poor" (Luke 7:22). After all, we pray "Thy kingdom come, Thy will be done in our neighborhood as it is in heaven." In the meantime, we host parties; we eat and drink with neighbors, and we see what work God will bring our way.

## Don't Trunk-or-Treat

*(Loving our neighbors radically changed our perspective on Halloween. The world looks different when you quit hiding and start playing offense.)*

October 30, 2013 by Joe Anderson

You're probably familiar with the various Christian approaches to Halloween. When I was a kid, my parents never took us trick-or-treating, not because of any major theological objections, but because we grew up in rural Kansas and our closest neighbors were about a mile away. It simply wasn't a part of the culture.

Of course, we knew of many Christians who objected to *any* kind of celebration of Halloween, not wanting to even acknowledge the holiday by doing something else. Others found that having an alternative, a fall festival or some such event, offered a Christian alternative for the youth group and kiddos in the church... that was probably an improvement over just having all the Christians stay at home that night.

Until we moved into our current home in Englewood, it never occurred to me that celebrating Halloween *by* trick-or-treating might actually be the most Christian option of all. From the day we moved in, our goal was to make our neighborhood our mission field and simply love our neighbors into the kingdom. We moved into our house in April of last year and by Halloween we knew the people who lived in perhaps 6 of the 19 homes on our block. Not a bad start, but a ways to go.

When Halloween rolled around, it occurred to us that we had an incredible opportunity to develop relationships with our neighbors. Halloween night, it turns out, is the only night in the year that your neighbors will happily greet you and your kids at their front door without any suspicion that you are a solicitor or have ulterior motives (other than to score a handful of candy-corn). Furthermore, on what other night will every parent in your neighborhood come, kids in tow, to your door to meet you?

So what did we do? We went trick-or-treating just on our block a little bit early. At each house, we went up to the door with our kids and introduced ourselves after the kids got their candy. We then hurried back home so we could hand out candy to everyone else who came by. Most parents with small children would stand down on the sidewalk while their kids came to our door. So, while my wife gave them candy, I walked down and introduced myself to their parents.

When questions of cultural engagement are considered in the abstract, the answers get skewed. "How should Christians relate to the world on Halloween?" ends up in one of two places—either separate from the world, or imitate the world's practices. When the question is reframed in terms of our mission, the answers are less lofty, more practical, and keep Christ at the center: "How can I best love my neighbors on Halloween?" For us, the answer was, "Go trick-or-treating." After all, we can't love our neighbors if we don't know them, and on that night, our neighbors were waiting for us to ring the doorbell. That night we doubled the number of names we knew on our block and many of those relationships have since flourished.

Now there are Christians — especially those who came to Christ from an occult background — who simply do not celebrate Halloween, and that's fine. Romans 14:5 has made it clear that there's a range of acceptable options for Christians here: "One person esteems one day above another; another esteems every day alike. Let each one be fully convinced in his own mind." But among the range of options available to conscientious Christians, one has lately grown popular that seems to be the worst of both worlds.

If you drive around Denver at this time of year, you'll see a lot of "Trunk-or-Treat" signs in front of churches. For those of you who are blissfully ignorant of this practice, trunk-or-treat is where you pack your trunk full of candy, dress your kids in Halloween costumes, and then drive them to the church parking lot, where they will go trick-or-treating from car to car, along with all the children of your Christian friends, who also showed up.

Obviously, trunk-or-treaters have no problems with the morality of Halloween. They're dressing their kids in costumes, going about begging for treats, the whole nine yards — everything that the popular culture around them does for Halloween. The only difference is that they're not doing it in their own neighborhoods, where they might build relationships with unbelievers — they're doing it with their Christians friends at church, where they have no impact at all on the world. If you serve in the kind of church where your trunk-or-treat event actually reaches your literal neighbors, great! Don't let us stop you. But if it's taking you out of your neighborhood on one of the few days you can meet your neighbors naturally—why would you do that?

## Who is my Neighbor Church?

*(In April of 2014, the Torrey Honors Institute at Biola University held a round-table discussion on "The Future of Protestantism" that made quite a splash in conservative circles. One of the key topics of conversation was the unity, or lack thereof, of Protestantism, and how we might better relate to communions both "closer" to our own and "further away" — these spatial words being defined exclusively in metaphorical terms. Our take? "Love your neighbor" is one of the big two commands. Although the command does legitimately extend by metaphor to cover about any situation, a large part of the command's power to give us a new perspective comes from taking it very literally, even when extending it into a domain like church relations.)*

May 9, 2014 by Joe Anderson

"But he, wanting to justify himself, said, 'And who is my neighbor?' And Jesus said to him, 'First, your neighbors are the people in your church, then the ones with whom you enjoy greatest doctrinal or ecclesiastical commonality, then those with whom you enjoy less commonality.'"

**-Said Jesus... never**

We made the case in a previous post that unity of all of God's people is internal to the gospel; God is making all peoples into one in Christ through His Church. With denominations in the multiple thousands and animosity between some branches of the tree going back a millennium or more...we have our work cut out for us. This is going to take a while.

Knowing that unity is central to our witness and internal to the gospel, we have to make a go at it. But where do we start? As we have observed this conversation unfold following the round-table discussion at Biola last week, we have noticed a serious blind spot on this point.

The conversation seems to have gone like this: Getting the Reformed churches and the Roman Catholic Church united would require unparalleled repentance on the part of the Roman Catholic Church, and that seems unlikely. Furthermore, the Reformed churches are entirely too fragmented as it is, so before we tackle unity with Rome, let's start at home, and try (for example) to unify the many Presbyterian denominations that are already in confessional agreement.

This sounds reasonable enough, and certainly it's a worthy objective. But let's take a closer look at that phrase "let's start at home." When Leithart says,[1] "Catholicity cannot begin at home, because, by definition, what happens at home isn't catholic," he is depending on a metaphorical definition of "home" (meaning one's "home" denomination or ecclesiastical tribe). Doug Wilson's discussion[2] of "local loyalties" does the same thing, using "local" to mean "nearest in confessional terms." The fact that the metaphorical is allowed to overwhelm the literal in this way exposes a significant blind spot.

---

[1] http://www.firstthings.com/blogs/leithart/2014/05/against-tribal-ecumenism

[2] http://dougwils.com/s16-theology/two-cheers-for-tribalism.html

Your neighbors are not principally the people who believe exactly what you do and live in another state. Your neighbors are the people who live 30 feet from your front door. As a church, your neighbors are... the people who live 30 feet from your front door. As a church, your neighbor churches are principally the ones right down the (non-metaphorical) street, not the ones that believe exactly what you do, and have an address in another state.

Of course, you have a duty to love your metaphorical neighbor churches (churches in your denomination that live in another state), but not at the expense of the church down the street. The churches two blocks away are your literal neighbor churches, and you have a Christian duty to tangibly love them. This is difficult to do if you never spend time with them or even learn the names of their people.

Catholicity, in fact, must begin at home, at your literal home, because Jesus said to love your neighbors. He didn't just mean unbelievers. Have some Christians from other churches over. Eat together, like Paul did and Peter (temporarily) didn't. Team up to love your unbelieving neighbors together, and see what happens. If you're a pastor, become friends with the other pastors in your city; you'll be surprised how much common ground you have and you'll find the blessing of local, catholic, friendship a great encouragement. A friend close by is better than a denominational brother far away, as Solomon might have put it.

# Stance of Blessing Articles

*Becoming more engaged with our neighbors is only a good thing if we have something good to offer them. Too often, the world just experiences our disapproval; we need to learn to bless what can be blessed.*

## The Thirteenth Clown

*September 19, 2013 by Tim Nichols*
*"We're going to duck into Perkins for lunch," the deputy said. I was riding along with an Osceola County sheriff's deputy as part of a class I was taking. It was after 11 pm, but I'd worked nights for nearly a year, and it didn't seem all that strange to me to call the midshift meal "lunch" no matter what time it was.*

*"My girlfriend's gonna bring my son out so we can have lunch together before he goes to bed." He explained, watching me out of the corner of his eye. He must have seen the reaction I tried to hide. "He's not her kid — had him with my ex-wife. But I guess you don't approve of divorce either."*

That's what the world sees when it looks at Christianity. It sees us taking a stance of moral arbitration. It sees us approving — or more often disapproving — based on how they adhere to our moral standards. Those standards can be silly (no piercings, except for one piercing in each earlobe, and only for women; no dyeing your hair unnatural colors, unless your hair is naturally grey) or they can be black-letter Bible (don't steal, don't have sex with anyone you're not married to). Of course it matters enormously to us whether our standards are God-ordained or just silly man made trash, but it doesn't matter at all to them.

What matters to them? That we have chosen to stand over them, to play the moral referee. Our compulsion to judge is so strong that we feel like we're somehow being unfaithful if we don't express our disapproval. A dear (male) friend of mine just started dating men a few months back. "I have friends who tell me every time I talk with them that they don't approve of my lifestyle," he told me. "I finally said, 'Look, I'm just going to assume that you haven't changed your mind until you tell me otherwise. Can we just stop talking about it?'"

Can we? Are we allowed to? As in all things, Jesus sets the example, and His example is most instructive.

John 8 tells how Jesus was teaching in the temple when a group of religious leaders appeared and threw down a woman in front of Him. "This woman was caught in adultery — in the very act!" they said. "Moses taught us that such a person should be stoned to death. What do you say?"

He didn't say anything. He didn't even look up. He just stooped down and began to write in the dirt. They kept asking, becoming more and more insistent. Eventually He just said, "Which one of you is without sin? That man can cast the first stone." Beginning with the oldest, they began to walk away, until finally they were all gone.

"Woman, where are your accusers?" Jesus asked.

"Gone," she said.

"I don't accuse you either," Jesus said. "Go and sin no more."

If we look at this case through the lens of our conventional evangelical "standing for truth," what do we see? Moses did say that someone committing adultery should be stoned to death. Jesus just didn't follow through. Why not?

In another case (you can read the whole story in John 4), Jesus refused to take sides in a theological dispute. "Our fathers worshiped on this mountain [Gerzim], but you Judeans say that one should worship in Jerusalem," the woman at the well said to Jesus. She is setting before Him a very old argument going all the way back to the days of Jeroboam the son of Nebat, who ruled over the ten northern tribes after the death of Solomon. Afraid that his people would not submit to his political rule if they continued to worship in Jerusalem, Jeroboam set up alternate locations for worship. The Samaritans had continued to worship in Gerzim right up into Jesus' time.

Now, there is definitely a right answer here. God ordained worship in Jerusalem, and Jeroboam's choice to worship in an alternative site was high rebellion. The Old Testament Scriptures make this very clear, repeatedly naming him as "Jeroboam the son of Nebat, who caused Israel to sin." But Jesus dodges the question. "Woman, believe Me," Jesus said, "The hour is coming when you won't worship the Father here or in Jerusalem either....The hour is coming — and it's here — when true worshippers will worship the Father in spirit and in truth, because the Father is seeking such people to worship Him" (John 4:23).

Another incident is even more stark (Luke 12:13ff).

"Teacher, tell my brother to divide the inheritance with me!" a man called out from the crowd. We know nothing about his situation. Was his brother swindling him out of his inheritance? Was he trying to swindle his brother and trying to get Jesus to help him put pressure on his brother to cave in? We have no idea. We do know what Jesus said next.

"Man, who made Me a judge and arbitrator over you?" (Luke 12:14).

Don't we want to argue with Him, just a little? He's God in the flesh, the only perfect man ever to walk the face of the earth. If He's not a fit judge, then who is? Yet He rejects the role of judge in this case.

We can struggle with when it might be appropriate to forego judgment, but one thing we can be sure of: if we *never* forego judgment, then we are doing it wrong. There were times when Jesus did. If we preach the gospel as Jesus did, we can be sure that there will be times when we should skip moral judgment in order to move on to more important matters.

Might this be such a time? At Headwaters, we think so. Jonathan Edwards delivered his classic sermon "Sinners in the Hands of an Angry God"[3] to a smug society secure in its own (self-)righteousness. In that milieu of genteel, churchgoing apostasy of the heart, the message of God's wrath against sin was a kiss on the lips. Convicted of their sin and their need for God, people fell on their faces in repentance and came to Christ by the thousands. In that day and time, "Sinners in the Hands of an Angry God" was good news.

By contrast, today we are a society saturated with disapproval. Deodorant commercials tell us how much

---

3   http://www.ccel.org/ccel/edwards/sermons.sinners.html

we stink.[4] Hair dye commercials tell us that nobody sees who we really are — just our grey hair.[5] A talking baby tells us what idiots we are about money.[6] We don't have the right clothes, the right car, the right retirement planning, the right credit score, the right anything. Approval is available, of course — for a price. Buy this deodorant, that hair dye, this car, get that investment plan, live in this neighborhood....

Pastor and author Doug Wilson has famously pointed out that when there are twelve clowns in the ring doing what clowns do, the tone is already set. It doesn't matter if you're out there reciting Shakespeare — if you get in that ring, to the audience you're just the thirteenth clown.

Contemporary man lives out his days against a backdrop of constant disapproval, of constant anxiety about not measuring up. In that milieu, a Christian disapproving of his moral conduct is just the thirteenth clown — another voice amid the hubbub.

That's hardly good news.

## Bless and Do Not Curse

*(Jesus laid an especially good foundation for His followers to take a stance of blessing toward the world, and this was not lost on His early followers. This article was one of our early attempts to lay out the Christian history of blessing.)*

*October 22, 2013 by Tim Nichols*

---

4   http://www.youtube.com/watch?v=UF4lAclHALc

5   http://www.youtube.com/watch?v=uloBZjYEym0

6   http://www.youtube.com/watch?v=783CfN2R18k

"Bless those who persecute you; bless and do not curse" (Romans 12:14). Paul wrote these words to the church at Rome. He had more reason than most to curse his persecutors: in constant peril from political intrigue and from plots on his life, was flogged almost to death five times, beaten with rods three times, stoned and left for dead — and those were just the high points. Why didn't he?

Paul had deeply personal reasons for his gracious attitude. He was there when Stephen was stoned, holding the coats of the men who killed him. In order to appreciate what happened there for Paul (then Saul), we need to think about who Stephen was, and what happened at his death.

Stephen was a man full of faith and power, a worker of miracles. Remember that the curse of such a man could result in death (Ananias and Sapphira) or blindness (Elymas). Had Stephen chosen to curse those who killed him, his curse would have carried considerable weight.

Remember also what Stephen saw, standing there in the judgment chamber. He looked up, the heavens were opened to him, and he saw Jesus standing at the right hand of the Father. More than one sermon has made much of the fact that Jesus was standing, since we know his usual position is seated (Eph 1:20, Heb 8:1, 10:11-12). The usual sentiment is something along the lines of Jesus giving Stephen a standing ovation, or standing in recognition of Stephen's faithfulness, or some such thing. These are interesting ideas, but they all suffer from the same significant hermeneutical flaw: they come from us superimposing our culture on the historical situation. Standing in recognition, or to applaud — these are things we would do.

But if we pay attention to our Bibles, there is an obvious alternative. Jesus is God in the flesh, enthroned in heaven. What is the biblical significance of God getting up from His throne? When God gets off His throne, somebody is about to get hurt. (See Pss 3:7, 7:6, 9:19, 10:12, 17:13, 68:1, 82:8) God gets up off His throne to vindicate the righteous and punish the wicked. If Jesus was following that pattern, then He stood up to act, to strike down the evil men who were about to murder His servant.

Saul of Tarsus could have died with the coats of the murderers in his arms.

Stephen could see it coming, and did the most amazing thing a human being can do: instead of crying out for God to destroy his persecutors, he said, "Lord, do not charge them with this sin."

God heard Stephen's merciful prayer. Saul of Tarsus survived, became Paul the Apostle, and the rest is history.

Even in his extreme situation, Stephen did not curse his accusers. How much less should we curse those whose sins are only afflicting us peripherally — yet we do.

For example, consider American Christians' relationship to Hollywood. We blame them for corrupting the youth, coarsening the culture, and pretty much any social ill that comes to mind. We speak ill of the folks in Hollywood at pretty much every opportunity. We fund ministries that will do the same, like "discernment" efforts that catalog every punch, every square inch of skin and every cuss word in a movie, often to the exclusion of discussing anything good about the film. We all recognize that if we call a kid stupid for his whole life, he's likely to think he's stupid, and act stupid as a result. But we think nothing of nattering on about how Hollywood is evil.

Contrast that to the approach of Mastermedia International, which mobilizes a global effort to hold up Hollywood leaders in prayer.

Which of these efforts, do you think, does Jesus approve of?

We don't think of ourselves as cursing other people, but how often do we let unwitting curses come out our mouths by saying things like...

"You always do this!"

"You never ____!"

"He'll never change!"

"That's just the way she is."

""With [the tongue] we bless our God and Father, and with it we curse men, who have been made in the likeness of God. Out of the same mouth proceed blessing and cursing. My brethren, these things ought not to be so." (Jas 3:9-10) Indeed, they should not. If you've been guilty of accidental curses of this kind, There's no time like the present to repent. You might pray something like this:

"Lord, I confess that I have made a habit of cursing people whom You created. It's so much a part of me that I'm hardly aware that I'm doing it. Please sensitize me to the things I say, and show me how to bless the people around me instead of cursing them. Amen."

## "Peace To This House"

*December 3, 2013 by Joe Anderson*

We want to dig a little bit deeper into what it looks like if we lay down our impulse to take a stance of moral arbitration and assume a stance of blessing instead. How did Jesus actually say to do it?

In Luke 10, Jesus appointed 72 disciples to go ahead of Him through the land of Israel. The instructions He gave them were remarkably simple.

"When you enter a house, first say, 'Peace to this house.' If someone who promotes peace is there, your peace will rest on them; if not, it will return to you… Heal the sick who are there and tell them, 'The kingdom of God has come near'" (Luke 10:5-6, 9, NIV).

"Peace to this house." Now, this was a common greeting of the time, but for Jesus and His disciples it went beyond a simple greeting. It was a test, a way of discerning the person they were talking to. Remember, these disciples were walking into towns where they didn't know anyone and didn't have anywhere to stay. This was by design. If someone received them after they were greeted with "Peace to this house," then the peace offered would rest on the house and they would know that the one who accepted them was a "person of peace."

Having a person of peace was their key to the city. In fact, Jesus told them not to go from house to house. Without a person of peace, they would have no ministry in a city, but with a person of peace, they could freely minister. This principle is actually pretty ingenious. If the disciples went into the city, set up camp and started preaching, they would have been dependent on their own charisma to carve out a hearing among the people. But if they developed a relationship with one willing gospel partner, they could use that person's pre-existing network of relationships to minister to others. It's a shortcut of sorts.

Now, Jesus could have told the disciples to enter the city and start with a public call of repentance. But He didn't. He could have told them to go to the synagogue and announce the coming of the Messiah. But He didn't. Nor did He take that approach in His ministry. What did Jesus do? He healed the sick, brought sight to the blind, and forgave sins. He brought a message of peace and told His disciples to do likewise.

How can we bring Jesus' message of peace to our neighborhoods, workplaces and the marketplace? It's nice to think about, but practically speaking, what do we do?

First, develop a discipline of greeting others. Too often, we have too many things going on to slow down long enough to really greet our neighbors. At most, we yell "Hey!" and wave without even breaking stride as we go from house to car, juggling a bag and a couple of kids, already late. That is not a greeting. **Stop** what you are doing. **Look** at the person you are greeting. **Attend** to that person. What is he saying? How does he look? **Ask** God what He wants to accomplish in this encounter that He has just given you. **Accept** that this will take time. **Pad** your schedule accordingly. That's right, folks: **SLAAAP** your neighbors.

Second, offer peace to them. Our natural tendency here is to individualize and customize:

what does it look like to offer peace to this particular person? What is he struggling with? What are the sources of conflict in his life? And so on. All that is well and good. We certainly should engage those questions. But before we jump to the metaphorical extension of what Jesus said, what if we just do what He said? What if we cultivate the discipline of literally blessing the person with peace?

"Mark, may God's peace rest on you."

"May the peace of Christ be with you today, Janet."

"Thank you for having us over. May God's peace be in this house."

Third, notice how they respond. Jesus told us that some people would respond to our offer of peace with peace, and others would not. The people who do are the ones God has prepared to respond to the ministry He has given us to do. These are the people through whom God will extend His Kingdom.

## Soft on Sin?

*(This column uses a popular music video from 2013 as a jumping-off point. Even if you liked the song, you've long since forgotten about it by now — one of the points we make, actually — but the same kind of analysis can be done with this year's favorites.)*

*January 10, 2014 by Tim Nichols*

*"Absolute good cannot be achieved in man's empirical existence — there is an element of imperfection in all human undertakings." - Archimandrite Sophrony,* Saint Silouan the Athonite

Over the last few months we've been writing here about taking a stance of blessing toward the world. In

"The Thirteenth Clown," we talked about how readily Christians default to a stance of disapproval and condemnation. We think we're standing for the truth, but in reality we're acting just like the rest of our culture — disapproving. In "Bless and Do Not Curse," we talked about, well, blessing the world rather than cursing it. In "Peace to This House," we explored one way of doing that in our encounters with our neighbors.

As we've talked about this topic with people, we mostly get one of two reactions. The vast majority of people are excited to see another way of relating to the world. They know that the stance of disapproval doesn't work, and yet they've felt themselves required to be that way. We have the pleasure of seeing God set these people free to love and bless their neighbors, which is just awesome. We love it. A significant minority, though, seem suspicious that we just don't care about the righteousness of God anymore. That we're giving up on standing for the truth. That we've gone soft on sin. This is *not* true — not remotely — but we understand why it can look that way.

In order to clarify a bit, we'd like to give you a real-time example of what we're talking about, one that you can all participate in yourselves. Fasten your seatbelts, folks, the ride might get a little rough.

Last year, the song "Cruise" by Florida Georgia Line broke records for the longest-running #1 country song ever. This was partly due to a change in the calculation methods, but it was also due to it being a *really* popular song, even before they did a remix version with Nelly. (Yes, *that* Nelly. The rapper.) The remix was popular as well, and...voilà. Longest-running #1 country hit ever.

Suppose you're talking with one of the neighbor kids, and he wants to show you this music video. He whips out his smartphone, and shows you the music video. (Go ahead — find it online and watch it all the way through.) If you're going to comment on it — which we'll ask you to do in a minute — have the courtesy to see it first.

The music cuts off. The last exhortation to "Get your radio up!" echoes and fades. The neighbor kid looks at you expectantly. *What do you say?*

Take a minute to think about it, and then we'll give you our take on it.

There's a lot we *could* say. Here are some of the things that occurred to us as we watched the video:

The music is trite, disposable pop. Forget. This kid won't even think about this song a year from now.

Every woman in this video is being displayed like a piece of meat in a butcher's window, an object for men to lust after.

In the scene where Nelly gets pulled over, my wife and I both noticed the nod to people getting pulled over for "driving while black." I thought it was funny; my wife thought it was tacky.

The lyrics. I could go on, but let's just take this bit: "this brand new Chevy with a lift kit/Would look a hell of a lot better with you up in it." The girl is an adornment for the dude's truck? Self-absorbed much?

It reminded me of Grady Smith's composite video of mainstream country songs of 2013,[7] in which he showed up a bunch of popular songs for what they were: different versions of the same bad pick-up line. (Watch; it's funny.)

---

7  http://www.youtube.com/watch?v=WySgNm8qH-I

These are all negatives. But there was one enormous, overwhelming positive thing about this video that hit me right away. *Two white country singers and one black rapper made it, together, and the fans accepted it.* Imagine someone attempting that in, say, Birmingham in 1963. Couldn't happen, as some of you well remember. Even within my own lifetime, I remember a time when that wouldn't have happened, when the latent racism in the fan bases on both sides would have cost everybody involved their careers if they'd dared to try. There are various sins being committed in this video, and a few assaults on good taste besides. But there's one sin that's *not* being committed, and it's a sin that was a defining part of our national character for a long time. The fact that such a collaboration is finally *possible* is very good news, and as with all good news, we ought to thank God for it.

Now, here's the question. As the neighbor kid looks expectantly at me for my reaction, all this floods through my mind. What do I say *first*?

Taking a stance of blessing means starting with gratitude. Begin by thanking God and go from there.

"You know, buddy, this video is way more amazing than you think it is. I remember a time when Nelly and Florida Georgia Line couldn't have worked together. They would have lost all their fans for working with him, just because he's black, and Nelly's fans would never have put up with him working with two white country boys. Crazy, right? It wasn't actually that long ago. Pretty cool that they can do it now, huh?"

Does that mean we don't talk about the other stuff? Of course not. Maybe we can go on from there to talk about some of those other points.

"Hey, that reminds me of this music writer, Grady Smith. He put together a mash-up of a bunch of this year's country music videos. He's making fun, kinda, but he also wrote a column about the 10 best country albums this year[8] — some of those songs are pretty good, too."

Here we get to talk about the numbing sameness of so many popular songs, and the originality on display in some of the better music.

Or...

"Hey, let's go back in that video; I want to show you something. Okay, pause it right there at 1:16. You ever see a real girl lean over and rub an engine that way, especially dressed like that? No? Hmmm...me neither. So why do you think they put it in the video?"

Here we get to have a conversation about sexual exploitation, about reducing real women to objects for masculine lust. If it goes well, we're even going to get to talk about how some girls really *will* act like that — they're so desperate for male attention that they'll emulate a music video if that's what it takes. If it goes *really* well, we'll get to move on to talking about what he can do to make sure his sisters and his female friends never, ever feel like they have to do that.

Or maybe...

"You like this song a lot, huh? Think back to this time last year...you were in, what, seventh grade? And you'd just gone back to school after Christmas...do

---

8   http://music-mix.ew.com/2013/12/18/best-country-albums-of-2013/

you remember what songs you were listening to a lot then?"

Either he can't remember, which is perfect, or he can remember a few, which is fine — I'll follow up.

"How often do you listen to those songs now? Do you think you'll still listen to them a year from now, or two years from now?"

Here we get to talk about the built-in obsolescence of pop culture, how it's made to be forgettable so you'll forget the old stuff and buy the new stuff...over and over again, a cycle designed for the sole purpose of separating him from his money. If that goes well, maybe we also get to talk about how some music doesn't go out of date. I'll use "House of the Rising Sun" as an example — the first recording of it was made in the thirties, and it was an old Appalachian folk song even then. Maybe we'll explore the different versions. Maybe we'll jump songs, and I'll teach him "Black is the Color of My True Love's Hair" or "Scarborough Fair." If I go with "Scarborough Fair," maybe I'll tell him the history of the song, and how it goes back to a much earlier, and much darker, song called "The Elven Knight." In any case, we'll have a chance to talk about what makes these long-lived songs different from "Cruise."

Maybe I get to have one or more of those conversations. *Maybe.* Maybe not. Maybe his mom calls, and he goes home for supper. Maybe he's so amped up on sugar, caffeine and hormones that it's near impossible to have a conversation, and I'm lucky to get a little gratitude in edgewise before he's off on the next topic. *It's okay. God is in charge of this.*

You see how this works? Taking a stance of blessing doesn't mean we can't talk about the bad stuff. It means that we start with gratitude to God. It means we don't allow other people's sins and imperfections to blind us to what we can be thankful for. What we can be thankful for, we can bless. We begin with blessing what can be blessed and proceed from there — and there's nearly always something to bless, if we have eyes to see it.

These same principles apply regardless of the situation. Jesus wasn't afraid to speak to sin, and we shouldn't be either — but we should pay attention to how He did it: "I don't condemn you either; go and sin no more." Notice which one comes first (see John 8 for the whole story).

A ninth-grade boy comes in and shows you an obscene rap video about a boy getting beat up by his dad. Of course, the video is liberally sprinkled with female dancers, their nubile bodies covered in just enough cloth to make a decent-sized cape for a hummingbird. But you look up at the end of the video, and there are tears in the kid's eyes. Are you going to chew him out about lust, or deal with why the video made him cry?

You meet your new neighbors, and discover that they are a pair of gay men in their 50s. They already know that religious people don't approve of them. Maybe you skip that part of the conversation and give them a plate of brownies, trusting God to bring up the issue in His time...*if He even wants you to do it.* Maybe He'll use someone else to have that conversation with them.

It's okay to notice all the things that God *could* do through you in a given situation. Maybe He will do some of them, but living as God's agent of blessing in the world is *not* about you doing the job. It's about trusting God to give the fruit *He* wants to give, when He wants to give it.

---

## Prayer Exercise

Blessing starts with gratitude, and gratitude starts with having eyes to see. Pray for eyes to see.

"Lord God, I confess that often I see the sin first, and I let the imperfections blind me to the good things that are also happening. Please open my eyes to see whatever is true, whatever is noble, whatever is lovely, whatever is of good report — anything virtuous and anything praiseworthy. Teach me to think on those things, to praise You for them, and to bless them in the world. I ask in the strong name of Jesus, who spoke many blessings over imperfect people during His ministry on earth. Amen."

For the next week, to take some time each day and list out five things you are thankful for that day. If that's too easy, once a day stop and list five things you're thankful for in the last hour. *Don't approach this as a task to be done.* Approach this as a chance to see God answer your prayer and open your eyes to things you wouldn't have seen a week ago. See what God will show you.

www.ingramcontent.com/pod-product-compliance
Lightning Source LLC
Chambersburg PA
CBHW071751080526
44588CB00013B/2212